Credible W

Paranormal Police Stories

Andy Gilbert

Acknowledgements

I am extremely grateful for the time people have given and for the trust they have put in me to tell their stories. I am also grateful for their honesty, good humour and understanding that some of the subject matter needed to be approached in a sensitive way. It takes courage to tell other people about extraordinary incidents that are very personal to those involved.

My thanks go to the following contributors Dave, Gordon, Keith, Scrib, Alan, Paul, Sid, Tom, Mike, Mark P, Mark S, Mark T, Neil, Pat, Gareth B, Gareth J, Carl, Lee, Andy, Aileen, Graham, Chris, John, Andrew, Cynthia, Gary, Stephen, Geoff, Jenny, Eddie, Colin, C.Doby, Mick, Samantha, Theresa, Leslie, Ian, Helen, Gerry and Jonathan.

Context and historical research by Andy Gilbert

Sincere thanks to national and local branches of N.A.R.P.O for their assistance in tracing people.

Cover photograph by Clare Bridges from Cohort4

All royalties from this book will be donated to Cherry Orchard Garden Scheme. This is a charity based at Burntwood Memorial Community Association, Staffordshire and it has a membership primarily made up of people with learning disabilities. The charity is a training and development facility for disabled gardeners to gain skills and confidence with the hope that they will then be able to assist other parts of the community. (Charity no.1154296).

Prologue

Whether it was parked up in a panda, sat in the back of a public order van or even stuck in an observation point carrying out surveillance duties, anyone who was unfortunate to have worked with me during my time as a police officer will know that my topics of conversation are somewhat limited. After arguing about music, football and who really was the best James Bond, in no particular order, I would often ask the question, 'Have you ever seen a ghost?'

I was genuinely surprised to find out how many people actually had and I was fascinated by the accounts that they gave me. I discovered during these conversations that some of these encounters and other unexplained incidents had happened while they were on duty, or were in some way connected to the world of policing.

In the United Kingdom, there have been only a few high profile paranormal incidents involving police witnesses. The Enfield Poltergeist in 1977, where the attending officers witnessed moving objects in the lounge of a house, is perhaps the most well known. The Stockbridge haunting in 1987, where two officers witnessed the presence of a Victorian figure next to their car, followed by their police vehicle then being struck by unseen objects, has also been reported upon and documented in great detail.

More recently in August 2016, there was significant media coverage of police attending poltergeist activity in Rutherglen, Scotland. Officers were called to a property after a terrified family - a mother and her teenage son - had endured two days of unexplainable disturbances that eventually forced them to move out. It was reported that the officers saw clothes flying across rooms, lights flickering on and off and even a pet

Chihuahua that was playing in the garden suddenly appeared on top of a 7-foot high hedge. Despite the media coverage, my attempts to speak to the attending officers by contacting Police Scotland proved unsuccessful. Interestingly, freedom of information requests submitted by journalists reveal that paranormal incidents are being reported to the police on a regular basis throughout the UK. Similar events to the incident that took place in Scotland are included in this collection.

In 2007 a colleague and I attended a report from a security guard that there were intruders at a newly built retirement home complex in Streetly, an area seven miles north of Birmingham. It was a large building containing individual apartments with a foyer and communal area. The security guard was a young lad who looked genuinely frightened when we arrived at the scene. No one had actually moved in yet and the building was in the final stages of completion. The guard told us that he had been standing in the foyer area when suddenly all the lights began going on and off continually.

When the security guard went to investigate, he saw an elderly couple ballroom dancing in the communal sitting room. He ran off and immediately called the police. We carried out a thorough search of the building and found no dancing couples and everywhere seemed to be locked and secure. There was little else we could do other than tell the security guard to call us if he had any further problems.

We both felt really sorry for the guy, as he seemed really frightened. A few nights later, we decided to call back and just make sure the security guard was okay only to discover that he had left the job. We obviously didn't mention what had happened to the new guard as we didn't want to alarm him but the incident did motivate and reignite my interest in the subject and I started to think about all those conversations that had taken place in the early hours.

I began speaking with friends and raised the subject through various social media networks. Predictably, several people contacted me to tell me they had seen spirits behind the bar in various police social clubs and a number of others felt that C.I.D volunteering to deal with a prisoner was in their mind a 'paranormal incident'.

As time progressed I discovered, after providing reassurance that my interest was genuine, that some people were willing to speak to me about something they had witnessed that they could not fully explain. Some of these accounts were very personal and I felt privileged that they were being recounted for the first time. I began receiving emails and letters about a wide variety of unexplained incidents. I spoke with people on the phone or met them in person to try and get as much detail and understanding as possible about each incident. A friend who had transferred to Western Australia Police has also contributed to this collection. We had met up for a drink when he came back to the UK for a visit and he told me about a strange incident that he had experienced in a police station on the other side of the world.

Naturally, many of the stories will originate from places where I have worked and from people I know. I doubt though, for example, Walsall is the paranormal centre of the universe but it does make you wonder that if a relatively small area like that can generate so many stories, how many more countrywide are actually out there, waiting to be told? I would encourage everyone to start asking their own family and friends, and like me, they will be surprised at what so many others have experienced.

We are all raised with a set of beliefs and values and throughout our lives we tend to surround ourselves and mix in the same social circles as people who share those very same values and beliefs. This is natural, so it can be difficult when faced with ideas or events that challenge our own way of

3

thinking. I would just ask that this book is read with an open mind. However much we think we know about the world around us, perhaps we don't know everything.

Whether it is an encounter with an angel sent to protect and guide or demons sent to terrify, phenomena that are witnessed and the way these incredible encounters impact upon people, are true mysteries of the human experience. I hope you find interest and enjoyment in the incidents recounted in this remarkable collection of true stories.

Andy Gilbert 2017

The Credible Witness

This is a collection of compelling accounts from members of the police family who have witnessed, or have intimate knowledge of, unusual and unexplained incidents. Throughout history, people have been witness to thousands of strange and mysterious events. Many of them can undoubtedly be explained as regular, everyday events that were simply misunderstood. However, there remains a large number that defy all logic, reason and scientific explanation.

The most sceptical researchers believe that all reported supernatural or paranormal events do have rational explanations. On the other hand, those who try to prove the existence of something unexplained agree that while some events do have rational explanations, others simply do not. Whether or not ghosts and unexplained encounters are real, many people find them fascinating. While no one has conclusively proven that ghosts do not exist, a number of alternative explanations about physical or psychological causes for strange experiences have been put forward. It is certainly an interesting battleground of opinion.

People can hallucinate or make a genuine mistake. Unidentifiable noises or a sudden physical feeling may also cause a person to be convinced that it was paranormal. Cold spots are a common phenomenon in old buildings that are thought to be haunted and people often describe sudden drops in temperature or a small area of coldness in an otherwise warm room. A thorough investigation can sometimes trace the cold spot to a specific source, like a draughty window or a chimney. The sensation of a lower temperature can also come from reduced humidity. In one study, the locations reported to be haunted were significantly less humid than those that were not, but it is also accurate to say that sometimes the feeling of sudden cold experienced by people cannot always be explained this way. There is a discernible difference between a cold draught and an instant drop in temperature to freezing point.

Despite all the credible research that does takes place, there are still an immeasurable number of incidents and witness accounts that do not fit the comfortable conclusion that what had taken place was a natural occurrence. No sound waves, no mirrors, no broken windows or noisy central heating systems- just genuine witnesses- experiencing something extraordinary, which cannot be explained.

A poll carried out by YouGov for the Association for the Scientific Study of Anomalous Phenomena in 2014 discovered that more than half of those taking part (52 per cent) said they believed in the supernatural, a marked increase on the two previous comparable studies, in 2005 and 2009, which both found a level of around 40 per cent. The survey also found that one in five people claimed to have had some sort of paranormal experience. The poll covered more than 2,000 people, and the figures were weighted to make the study representative of the population. (Source, the Telegraph)

When an investigation is carried out, the investigator must use critical thinking and problem solving skills to figure out what really happened in a case. Critical thinking skills also allow the investigator to look past the obvious solutions and analyse evidence objectively. The contributors to this book are all intelligent people with considerable life experience. Many are also skilled and capable investigators within the police but when trying to provide a rational reason for the incident that they witnessed, they simply cannot. As any investigator will testify, a credible eye witness is often the strongest evidence of all and I would categorise every person who has taken part in this project as being a 'credible witness'. In several cases, they have been alongside colleagues who can provide corroboration of what took place.

Police work involves a search for the truth and establishing facts. Apart from the Professional Standards Department, investigators have to have evidence before they can draw a conclusion. Suspects often concoct stories and alibis that are beyond belief. Some attempts to explain away criminal actions border on fantasy, and fantasy is also a running theme in the propaganda churned out from internal police communications departments, contradicting what those working at the front line know to be true. You don't necessarily join the police with a cynical outlook upon the world, but the majority of those who work in a police environment, tend to leave with one.

The culture in policing and the personality traits of those involved have been analysed in a varied range of academic research, much of which provides critical arguments about the cynical features of police personalities. Police culture, and the cynicism that accompanies it, can be seen as an aspect of a police officer's personality which can be drawn upon at times when dealing with emotive and dangerous situations. It could be argued that cynicism can provide officers with some protection from feelings of being gullible or stupid. What makes this collection of accounts interesting is that they are being told from a culture and environment where matters such as these are rarely discussed for fear of ridicule or the damage that could be caused to a person's professional reputation. Being sceptical can be a desirable professional trait, the ability to remain unconvinced until presented with hard evidence, whereas cynicism is an outlook on life. For those burdened with such an outlook, it must be pointed out that no one has gained financially, or in terms of personal kudos in helping with this book but the contributors have shown generosity and an understanding that some stories are just so interesting that they need to be told.

In recent years there have been wide scale reforms and cuts to the police budget and this has unsurprisingly reduced the capability of the police to respond to the most serious and demanding crimes. The consequence of reducing police numbers is that the scope for proactive work, aimed at protecting the most vulnerable people in our society, is diminishing. This has lead to police stations being closed down and sold off, and with them disappears a great deal of history and tradition, such as being able to walk into a police station for help any time of the day or night. Several of the stories in this book have taken place in old stations which are no longer in use.

These days a single-crewed officer drives from an incident requiring an immediate response, to another equally urgent situation with barely a chance to draw breath, so the lone officer patrolling on foot through the night has become a thing of the past. Occurrences witnessed during the nocturnal wanderings of beat Bobbies, as would be expected, make a significant contribution to this book.

It might be helpful to explain and discuss some of the accepted ways in which paranormal incidents are categorised and where some of the stories in this unique collection most comfortably fit.

Ghosts

A ghost is thought to be the spirit of a dead person that is dwelling between the two realms of the spiritual and the physical. They are strongly attached to the living realm by some emotional force. Descriptions of ghosts can vary widely from an invisible presence to translucent or barely visible shapes, to realistic, lifelike visions. Ghosts are typically identified as spirits that have not moved on, whereas spirits are often used to classify those who have crossed over. There are some differences between encountering a ghost and a spirit.

Usually spirits make you feel calm, comforted and reassured and a spirit also has the ability to come and go as it pleases.

Ghosts are often attached to a person or a place and bring with them an eerie feeling although there are cases of people living in the same place as a ghost and getting along fine together. I would imagine it is just like having children or pets in that you have to set boundaries. In the absence of a rational explanation, any doors, cupboards or drawers that seem to open on their own, lights switching themselves on and off, televisions or radios switching on and off, changing channels, or increasing in volume-could also indicate a spiritual presence.

Residual haunting

A residual haunting is believed to be caused by traumatic past events that leave an imprint on the environment. These imprints replay over and over, just like watching a DVD on permanent play. There is no interaction with the living and the activity would take place whether or not there was a witness present. It is thought that this sort of haunting is caused by the energy expended during repetitive or traumatic events. The energy is absorbed and stored in the electromagnetic field at the location and over a period of time the energy builds up. When the energy can no longer be contained it is discharged, showing a replay of the traumatic event that once took place. Once the event is played out, then the cycle begins again although the actual pattern and timing of the haunting can be hard to establish.

The energy may dissipate from one place to appear or exist in another; it can also reappear in a different form. Some scientists believe that this type of energy can suddenly discharge and play itself at various times. The events are not always visual either and can be replayed as sounds and noises that have no explanation. The audible footsteps or distant screams that are reported in many haunted places are good examples of this.

Historical haunting

Ghosts can be seen in more than one location, going about their business. Usually they are dressed in period clothing and often appear in a solid form. They sometimes interact with the living, but the ghost believes that they are living in their own time and can suddenly disappear.

Intelligent haunting

An intelligent haunting can be described as a presence that can communicate with you, and interact with you in a seemingly deliberate and intelligent way. It is usually a human entity with whom communication takes place. The ghost appears as the personality of a person who once lived, and who is either stuck in our world or has the ability to move between the physical and the spiritual at will. The personality of the ghost will reflect the personality it had when it was in human form, so it is probably better to meet an entity who was a decent person as opposed to someone who was unpleasant when they were alive. An intelligent ghost will be an attention seeker, moving objects making noises or displaying anti social behaviour. The key factor in an intelligent haunting is that the ghost can interact with you. If the ghost does not notice you or interact with you, it is not an intelligent haunting.

Shadow people

Shadow people refer to the possible paranormal apparition, which appears as a dark human-form manifestation or a larger solid black mass.

A shadow person may simply be a ghost that does not have the energy to fully manifest itself or it could be a spirit carrying a strong negative emotion, such as anger, sadness, or even hatred. This negative emotion can cause their energy to be darkened. There have also been many sightings of shadow animals.

Mists

Some apparitions may appear as a dark or a light mist that forms out of nowhere and then disappears just as quickly. In some cases, the mist assumes a full or partial human form. Many natural explanations may exist for mists, so it is essential to be certain it is not due to environmental conditions before suspecting paranormal activity.

Poltergeist

A poltergeist is a type of ghost or other supernatural entity which is responsible for physical disturbances, such as loud noises and objects being moved or destroyed. They are usually mischievous and sometimes malevolent and are purportedly capable of physically assaulting people. Witnesses to poltergeist activity describe the movement or levitation of household objects and furniture. Poltergeists are often troublesome spirits who haunt a particular person instead of a specific location.

Being watched

People who have witnessed ghost sightings frequently report experiencing powerful sensations such as the feeling that they are being watched, even when no one else is present. Other sensations reported include a feeling of not being wanted, or a strong feeling that they must leave a certain place immediately. Gut instinct is probably one of the best tools for being aware that something is not right.

Being Touched

Experiencing physical contact from a spirit, ghost or other paranormal entity would obviously be very frightening. The contact can be as simple as a tug on your clothing or pressure on a part of your body. In more extreme cases, people have reported being kicked or punched. Fortunately, serious physical injury in reported cases is rare.

The last moment of mortality

This is ghostly manifestation that occurs when someone is at the exact moment of their death. Some people believe it is the spirit or soul leaving the body. An apparition can also appear to a close friend or family member a great distance away

U.F.O's

There is a great deal of scepticism about the sighting of Unidentified Flying Objects and an opinion that there is a natural explanation for every single reported UFO seen in the sky. Numerous sightings are investigated and found to be nothing unusual. They turn out to be shooting stars, weather balloons, genuine aircraft or even Chinese lanterns. Perhaps a more accurate description would be 'misidentified' as opposed to 'unidentified' but there are still a significant number of sightings that cannot be explained. Even the Ministry of Defence would have to admit that there are some fascinating cases on their files that they have yet to resolve and sightings are still being reported on a regular basis. Again, despite all the research there are still conflicting views among scientists and academics.

At the moment, life on Earth is the only known life in the universe, but there are compelling arguments to suggest we are not alone. Indeed, most astrophysicists accept a high probability of there being life somewhere else in the universe. I mean, it is so enormous surely there has to be and one day we may well find that there is 'something' out there. Despite a lot of research in outer space, scientists have not yet been able to find evidence of life forms on any other planet but imagine if a similar planet to Earth had discovered the wheel a hundred years earlier than us and then made significant scientific discoveries at a faster pace. They could have developed the ability to travel and visit other planets and maybe this is the case with UFO's, although with so much conflict and stupidity on our planet, it is no wonder they don't stay long.

One:
Incidents on Foot Patrol

George Street, Walsall, West Midlands

What I am about to tell you took place when I was a probationary constable, posted to Walsall police station in the early 1980s. Walsall is a large town in the Black Country with a market area in the centre. The town is famous for its saddle making and leather industry.

I had just returned from two weeks leave and would be starting a set of seven nights, with the first one being on a Monday night. I was posted to foot patrol on the town centre and although not as warm as Majorca from where I had just returned, it was a pleasant summer night.

It was usually quiet at the start of the week and it got busier as the weekend approached. On this particular night, once the pubs had closed, it was a fairly routine patrol, checking the security of the shops and stopping to speak to anyone who happened to be walking about in the early hours.

A short time after midnight, I was walking along George Street when I suddenly saw a boy aged about thirteen, wearing school uniform, just a few yards ahead of me. My initial thought was, 'what the fuck is he doing out at this time of night?' Before I could think anything else, he ran straight towards me, so it was my intention grab hold of him and speak to him. The boy was running at quite a pace, so I put my arms out to grab him by the shoulders as he was coming straight towards me. I braced myself for the impact but felt nothing. The boy ran straight through me, not around me or to the side of me, but straight through my body.

I stood in shock, unable to move, staring at my boots where the boy should have been standing firmly in my grasp. By the time I turned around to look behind me, he had disappeared. I recognised the school uniform as being from one of the local schools in Walsall.

I was absolutely stunned and walked around for a while, trying to understand what had just happened. Later, I met up with another probationer who was also on foot patrol in the town centre. I told him what had happened, whether he believed me or not I don't know but I was relieved to tell someone. We both thought it was best not to mention it due to the culture in the police. If I had told my supervisors they would have thought I was insane. I finished my duty and went home, still thinking about what had happened and unable to make any sense out of it.

The following night on parade, the shift inspector announced that he wanted to speak to me in his office. If you are asked to speak with the inspector after parade it usually meant a bollocking was coming your way. I felt very uneasy because this particular inspector had a fearsome reputation. I walked into his office, anticipating the worst and the inspector opened the pleasantries with a brusque, 'Why didn't you find him?'

'Find who sir?' I responded.

The inspector then angrily informed me that earlier in the afternoon, the body of a schoolboy had been found on some wasteland near the town centre, and for obvious reasons I won't go into the specific detail, but sadly it looked like he had taken his own life. The deceased lad had attended the same school as the boy who had ran through me. It looked like his body had been at the location where it was found for a few days.

The inspector quizzed me further; he wanted to know if I had been on the wasteland the night before, which I hadn't. The inspector seemed very critical about not finding the body but it was just wasteland and not the kind of area that would warrant any attention, not when you have a large town centre to look after. I obviously didn't mention what had happened to me.

I left the office and was lost for words. The incident is as clear in my mind today as the same night that it happened and even today, I often think about that unfortunate boy.

King Street, St Leonards, East Sussex
I joined Hastings Borough Police in 1958, and after three months learning the beat with other officers, I was patrolling streets on my own. One night, on a 2200-0600 shift, I was allocated a beat in St Leonards-on-Sea, known locally as just St Leonards. The town has been part of Hastings, East Sussex, since the late 19th century though it still retains a sense of separate identity.

In those days we had no radios, so we made a certain 'point' every half hour and we rang in from a police box every hour. We notified our route to the telephone operator at the police station each time we rang in. I had made a point at the railway station in Kings Road at 0200; this was a fairly long road with shops on both sides. In those days the shop doors had to be checked for security, which I had just done. I was waiting at the 'point' and looked up Kings Road where I saw a policeman in a cape walking along the pavement towards me. I thought it was my sergeant coming to meet me and record it in my pocket book. He was walking in and out of the shop doorways, trying door handles. I initially thought that was little strange because that was not the sergeant's job, it was the job of the constable and I had just checked all the same doors that this police officer was now doing. Halfway down the street he went into a doorway and did not come back out, so I walked up the road to meet him. When I reached the shop doorway there was no sign of him whatsoever; I checked all around the immediate area but

15

there was no sign. He had walked into a doorway and disappeared, and bear in mind I knew for a fact that all these doors were locked, having just physically checked them.

At 0300 I went into the police station for my refreshments and spoke to my Sergeant who informed me that he had not been in that part of town at that time. I then spoke to the PC on the adjoining beat who told me that he was well away from my beat at that time also, so I told him what I had seen. He just laughed and said, 'I reckon you have seen the ghost of a PC who dropped dead in that road whilst working nights.'

To this day I wonder who or what I did actually see that night but on the police roll of honour there is an entry for a PC John King who died in July 1955, aged 38. PC King collapsed and died in St Leonards, shortly after reporting for night duty. Maybe my colleague was right and I did see John, finishing his last patrol, coincidentally walking along a road that shared his name.

The gates of St Peter and Paul, Aston, Birmingham

One winter around 1981, I was on nights and posted to foot patrol in Aston, Birmingham. It was quite a cold evening and there was a clear sky as I wandered round the seemingly never ending streets of terraced houses in the area.

I was walking along Trinity Road, having just passed the Aston Villa football ground and I was on the opposite side of the road to the Holte Pub. Just across the park on my right hand side was Aston Hall, a magnificent Jacobean mansion and a place of historical interest.

As I walked along I had a good view of the Aston Parish church (St. Peter and St. Paul), which is an imposing church with an impressive spire that can be seen from many parts of the Aston area, including the A38 and even from the M6 motorway.

I did not tell any of my colleagues when I returned to the station, simply because I didn't think they would believe me but I did tell my wife about it as soon as I got home. It really shook me up at the time and recalling the event now, even after all these years, it is quite emotional. You understandably don't forget when you see something like this.

Authors note

There has been other reported paranormal activity in Moor Lane. In 1996 a plumber on 24 hour call was travelling along Moor Lane past the cemetery at about 12.50am when he saw a man appear in front of his vehicle causing an unavoidable collision. When the driver stopped there was no trace of the pedestrian or any damage to his vehicle. The shocked driver reported the incident at Queens Road Police Station and the story featured in both the Birmingham Evening Mail and Birmingham Post. (source www.roadghost.com)

Probably the most well known 'ghost hunter' in recent times is Andrew Hunter, who passed away in 2004. Mr Hunter wrote several books on the subject of ghosts and carried out many investigations. In his 1980 book 'Ghosts of Today,' he includes two separate sightings of a man dressed in an RAF uniform, who vanished into thin air in Moor Lane.

Two:
Mobile Patrol

North of Birmingham

I started out my service working at police stations a few miles outside of Birmingham. After two years of either being on foot patrol or a passenger in police vehicles, I passed my driving course and was allowed drive a police car.

This incident happened soon after I had qualified as a police driver. I have deliberately omitted some of the details out of courtesy for other people who were involved in the incident or may have been affected by the events that I am about to describe.

It was at a time when cars were frequently being stolen, mainly for joy riding, to such an extent it had become a serious problem for the police. Many of the people who stole the cars seemingly enjoyed being chased by the police and had little regard for their own safety or the safety of anyone else. There was an expectation, that irrespective of your police driving experience, you would do your best to follow stolen cars and try and catch the offenders. It was often cat and mouse stuff, and on nights when the streets were relatively empty, pursuits with stolen cars took place all the time.

On this particular occasion, my partner and I were on mobile patrol in the north of Birmingham when a call came over the radio stating that a stolen car was being pursued about five miles away from our location. Naturally, I began to head towards the area where the pursuit was taking place. I was only a basic driver in an Austin Maestro panda car. There were two Austin Rover Montego area cars behind the stolen car that were being driven by advanced drivers. In all honesty, I did not really expect to get near to the real action but as we were travelling south, I saw the stolen car coming towards me pursued by the two area cars, lights flashing, sirens sounding.

I managed to get behind the other two police vehicles, trying to keep up but occasionally falling behind a little. Through the twists and turns of the streets, I caught sight of the stolen car ahead of me, racing at speed in a desperate attempt to get away.

The high speed convoy arrived on a notorious road for accidents, due to its snake like bends and corners. As the stolen car raced toward a junction, I saw the rear wheels leave the road surface causing the car to start rolling over. It seemed to be in slow motion as it flipped over and would have continued rolling, except that the roof smashed into a lamppost stopping the car dead, flattening the roof. The lamppost, damaged by the force of the impact, fell over landing directly on the car. The other police cars came to a stop past the wreckage, just ahead of me.

Seconds after the roof of the car had struck the lamppost, I saw a person get out of the passenger side and run straight across the road in front of me, causing me to slam on the brakes as he was lit up by my headlights and I just managed to avoid hitting him. I then saw the person run away over the road in front of me and he disappeared into the darkness of a large grassy recreation area. I immediately recognised the person as someone I had arrested recently and I had a good view of him in my headlights. The police officer I was with saw the lad as well and he also knew him by name.

I stopped my car and ran over to the crushed vehicle, as the priority was to establish if anyone else was inside the car that needed our help. The roof was crushed flat and it was impossible to see inside. I called up on the radio naming the person and informing the controller that the suspect had escaped across into the recreation area.

There was then some confusion as the officers who had been at the front of the pursuit came running over to me and said that no one had got out of that car and neither could they have. I insisted that my partner and I had both seen someone get out of the car and I again named the person who I thought it was, but they did not seem to be interested. This was obviously frustrating and at the same time confusing.

The fire brigade responded quickly to the incident and when they arrived they soon managed cut of the roof of the vehicle. As the twisted and crushed metal was cut away, there was only one person inside who had tragically lost their life. Because of the extent his injuries, it was difficult at first to recognise the person but a few moments later his identity was confirmed and when I heard the news I started to physically shake. The deceased person inside the car was the same person that I had seen run from the car in front of my panda, causing me to brake.

I spent a long time after that night questioning what I had seen but I was not alone, my partner saw it too although he started to doubt himself after a while. Nothing has changed in my mind, this happened over 25 years ago and I am still convinced that I saw that person get out of a stolen car and the person I saw get out was the deceased driver.

Whatever it was I did see on that night, I will let you decide for yourself.

Whitley, Coventry

In the early 1990's I was a PC on nights in Coventry, posted to a panda covering the Whitley area. I was single crewed driving an Austin Maestro. Whitley had its own identity based around a grand house that used to be there. Contrary to popular belief, the house which bore the name "Whitley Abbey" was not actually a monastic residence. Ironically though, there was a pub nearby that was for some reason called 'the Mysterious Monk'.

It had been a fairly quiet and uneventful night. At the bottom of Abbey Road was a place where stolen cars were often dumped, probably because it was fairly secluded at the point where it became a dead end. Vehicle security was not so great then and stealing cars was fairly easy. It was a popular pastime for the less law abiding member of the community.

It was a clear night and about three or four in the morning when I decided to drive down Abbey Road and see if my luck was in with regard to catching some car thieves or at least recovering someone's pride and joy. As I drove down the road I was surprised to see something in the middle of the road moving directly towards me. My first reaction was 'What the hell is that?' The object moved closer and closer, appearing to glide at a smooth and constant speed. I then realised that I was a looking at a monk in a brown habit but the manifestation had no face and no feet and levitated straight over the police car and disappeared out of my sight.

I could not believe what I had just seen and went straight back to the nick to try and gather my senses together. I told a couple of other officers on my shift who were in the station and they just laughed but I knew that I had just witnessed something out of the ordinary.

The incident didn't stop me going back as I still had a job to do and stolen cars were still being abandoned in the area although fortunately for me, I never saw the faceless monk again.

Wightwick Manor near Wolverhampton

In the mid 1990s I was working at Wolverhampton police station. I was double crewed with another officer on an area car, which at the time was an Austin Montego. It was a warm summer's night and we had the windows wound down on the car as we drove around patrolling our patch.

We travelled down the hill at Wightwick Bank towards the Bridgnorth Road, near to the Mermaid Public House. Situated here is a National Trust property known as Wightwick Manor (pronounced 'Wittick'). It is a very impressive building and for many years was the home of the Mander family. For over two hundred years the Mander family held a prominent position in the Wolverhampton area. The Mander family was a major employer in the town and their business became one of the largest printing ink manufacturers in the country. Members of the family were involved in civic affairs and several of them became mayor or served as aldermen. The family was also well known for its public services and philanthropic acts.

At this location there is a wooden arched bridge which traverses the old road and we were heading towards the section of road that would take us underneath the bridge. As we came very close to driving underneath, a female figure came into our view on the bridge. She was dressed in a long white Victorian style dress and was wearing a bonnet style hat. The lady was walking across the bridge, I say walking but I could not see her legs and her movement was so smooth it would be better described as gliding. The lady was just approaching the half way point on the bridge, so she still had a fair way to travel before she got to the other side.

My colleague, who was driving at this point, immediately stopped the police car just after we had passed underneath the bridge and we immediately looked at each other, seeing the shock in each other's face. We both then looked back onto the bridge but the woman had vanished.

There was absolutely no way, in the time it had taken us to stop the car and look back, that the woman could have made it to the other side of the bridge. There was no doubt from either of us as we spoke about what we had just witnessed. We both knew that we had just seen a ghost.

Chadwick End, Warwickshire

In the mid 1960s I was a member of the Solihull traffic department. I was working nights with a colleague travelling along the A41 approaching the village of Chadwick End. Chadwick End is approximately 6 miles south-east of Solihull town centre and is in the parish of Balsall. The village is not a traditional village in terms of houses situated around a village green with a church and a pub. It is best described as a crossroads settlement that has expanded over time, with a ribbon of development along the A41.

At about 0100 we were travelling along and we were negotiating a slight left hand curve by the gates to Chadwick Manor. In our headlights we luckily picked up a group of 5-6 nuns walking on our side of the road with their backs to us. Not only was it a real surprise to see a group of nuns, the situation was extremely dangerous, with them all being dressed in black, so we pulled round in front of them and stopped.

Despite how strange it was to see them, it was our intention to tell the nuns that it would be considerably safer if they walked the other side of the road, facing the oncoming traffic. At least the traffic could then pick up the white frontal parts of their habits. We had pulled up about thirty feet past the group of nuns and both got out of our vehicle. As we walked back to go and speak with the group we could not see them. They had completely disappeared.

We radioed through to control and explained what we had seen before searching the surrounding area, especially the driveway to Chadwick Manor to see if the nuns had walked along there. There was no sign of anyone in the area. The control room had put us on 'talk through' so other patrols had heard our transmissions about the incident.

The Warwick car was further along the A41 at Five Ways, half a mile or so the other side of Chadwick End village. They suddenly radioed in saying they had just passed the nuns who were still walking on the wrong side of the road. Just like us they stopped but by the time they got out of their vehicle the nuns had disappeared again. An incredible event that had been seen by four police officers had taken place yet there was no logical explanation for it.

The whole event was formally logged as a police incident by the control room but cannot be explained. It is also logged on the database of the British Paranormal Society and has featured in a book about ghosts in Warwickshire.

Catherine-de-Barnes Lane, Solihull

In the early hours of the morning around 1988, I was with another PC called Andy, travelling along Catherine de Barnes Lane towards Solihull. The name Catherine-de-Barnes derives from Ketelberne, a 12th century lord of the manor. The village has been known colloquially since the 19th century as Catney Barnes, often abbreviated to Catney. I was driving quickly as we were responding to a crime in progress and had the blue lights in the front grill of our unmarked white Rover illuminated. What I was about to witness only lasted for a few seconds but the memory of it is still clear.

The road we were on was surrounded by rural countryside, a long straight road. The road was lined by hedges and fields and there was no street lighting. As we raced past the junction with Shadowbrook Lane, about 25 metres ahead of me, I saw a man on horseback cross the road in front of us from right to left. Immediately I knew this was not a real person in the physical sense and I was witnessing something extraordinary.

The man looked like a highwayman as he was wearing a black flowing gown, and a black floppy hat, moving quickly yet gracefully. There were no field entrances or gates so he either jumped the hedges or had travelled straight through them. As the man had come into view, I had instinctively dabbed the brakes, and as we passed the point where the horseman had past in front of us I looked at Andy and then looked in the mirrors to see if the man on horseback had reappeared.

I think the best way to describe the expression on Andy's face would be a, 'What the fuck!' kind of look. I said to Andy, 'What was it?' To which he replied in his Black Country accent, 'Mon on a hoss.' This confirmed to me that I wasn't going mad because he had clearly seen the same thing as me, without any prompting or suggestion.

We continued at speed to the incident, both shaking our heads and now discussing what we'd seen. We were both stunned but did not have time to dwell on it because of what we were doing and the urgent job we were going to but when we had a quiet moment later on in the shift, we did speak about it in more detail. There was no doubt with either of us that we had seen a ghost of some kind.

We were parked up towards the end of the shift and a car from Eastern traffic stopped for a chat. One of the guys told us there was a history of highway men in the area and that one of them had been hanged. Being cynical, I wondered whether or not he was taking the piss as I would imagine there were criminals hanged all over the area centuries ago. When we arrived back at Park Lane to book off, our colleagues thought that we were the ones really taking the piss when we told them what we had seen, but that's just the way the culture is in the police.

Highworth, Wiltshire

I was a dog handler in Wiltshire and I usually patrolled alone but on this particular night I had another officer with me. During the early hours of the morning it had gone quiet and we were travelling from Swindon to Highworth for a brew with the local officers. Highworth is a small market town often described as the gateway to the Cotswolds.

I was driving the van and it was a warm summer night. Visibility was good and the road was clear with no other traffic about. On the approach into Highworth the road is straight and it slopes downwards before going uphill as you enter into the town.

I do not know the exact speed we were travelling at but we were not in any rush as everything was relaxed. The relaxed feeling changed instantly when from out of nowhere a column of what I can only describe as a dense vapour, suddenly reared up from nowhere in front of the van on the near side. I instinctively reacted and swerved to avoid whatever it was.

'Did you see that?' my colleague asked. I confirmed I had, although my evasive action should have made it obvious.

'What do you think it was?' I asked him. The immediate reply was, 'a ghost' which was exactly what I thought as well.

A little shaken, we turned back immediately and checked the road for some distance, several times. There was no sign of the vapour and no roadside drain at the point the vapour had appeared. The location had a wide grass verge giving us a clear view of the surrounding area, but we found nothing to explain our experience. The temperature or weather was not conducive to any mist, and anyway this was distinctly different.

We continued to Highworth, and knowing the police culture well, I advised my colleague to keep the matter between us. Upon entering the station, my partner could not contain himself and blurted out details of the whole incident. To my surprise, the two officers listening remarked that there had been fatal accidents on that road and they were very matter of fact about it.

During my service I have travelled that road many times, at all hours throughout the year but I never saw anything like it again despite always slowing down whenever possible. To this day I can offer no explanation as to what we saw but in the absence of any logical reason, I remain convinced that my initial reaction was right. We had seen a ghost.

Three:
Haunted Stations

Aldridge Police Station, West Midlands

I was promoted from constable to sergeant in the year 2000 was and posted to Aldridge Police Station. Aldridge is a quiet, prosperous suburb of Walsall with its own centre, consisting of shops, restaurants and pubs.

Having just spent ten years investigating serious crime on the CID, this seemed like a very nice place to be stationed. The station is an old building and still mainly in the same form as when it was constructed and is ideally placed on Anchor Road.

Parade time on nights was at 2200 and when this was over the team would go out on patrol. If it was not too busy, I would usually complete a couple of hours of paperwork in the sergeants' office. This meant that I was often alone in the station. The sergeants' office was on the ground floor and at one end of the station, the officers parade room was at the other end.

I was sitting at my desk writing away, when all of a sudden the room became very cold. The coldness was coming from directly behind where I was sitting. I looked around the office and established that there were no windows open. I felt a distinct chill go through me and I decided to investigate further. I looked around the room again and everything was as normal, the radiators were off as it was late summer.

I sat down at my desk again but I still felt uncomfortable so I went out of the office and walked down the corridor. The first thing that I noticed was that the air was considerably warmer, I walked on along the corridor and felt at ease again, the atmosphere, or whatever it had been that caused the cold feeling, seemed to be gone.

I returned to the office and sat down at my desk and carried on with the pile of paperwork but after a few minutes it began happening again, I felt a very cold chill coming from behind me, the temperature in the room had suddenly dropped and it felt like mid winter. It was making me feel very uneasy but I decided to carry on writing. I then noticed out of the corner of my eye that the coat stand that was in the corner of the room, which was covered in coats, started shaking for a few seconds and then stopped. I thought I must be seeing things, so again I got up looked around the office but found nothing amiss.

I was feeling a little spooked and I went outside into the corridor again. Once again, the air temperature was normal, I walked through the building and everything felt fine. There was still no one in the building except for me. I thought this must be some form of prank and returned to the office and looked at the coat stand, there was nothing attached to it and there were still no windows open.

I attempted to return once again to work. This time everything seemed fine and I worked for an hour or more feeling comfortable. Just as I was going to get up and make a drink, the freezing cold air behind me returned and the temperature of the room dropped rapidly. There was a real feeling of dread in the air. I started to turn my head and as I did I saw the coat stand starting to shake backwards and forwards as if some invisible hand had taken hold of it. The coat stand then flung itself onto the ground, the coats falling off it as if someone had thrown it over with deliberate force.

I left the office and went quickly down the corridor to find some of the officers had returned for their refreshment break and they were sitting playing cards in the parade room. When I told them what had happened they laughed but they came with me and saw the coat stand lying on the floor for themselves.

I have never been able to explain what happened that night, these things stay with you. You won't be surprised to hear that I spent as little time as possible on my own in the station after that night and although it never happened again, I moved the coat stand into a corner and put a chair up against it whenever I was in the office on my own at night.

(2) In the spring of 2013 I was stationed at Aldridge nick working on a response team. There were a three of us on nights at Aldridge with the rest of the response team working at the main parade station situated a few miles away in Walsall. There is no 24/7 enquiry office so the only people coming in and out of the nick during the night would be the response officers that I had paraded with.

I was single crewed and had to pop back into the nick during the early hours, I can't actually remember what for, it could have been for a piss or to collect some statement paper but I knew that there would be no-one else in the building because I could hear on the radio that the other Aldridge officers were committed at incidents.

I drove through the coded barrier and into the back yard. There were no other cars there and I parked up and started walking towards the back door. As I was walking I glanced up at the first floor window above the sergeants' office and saw the silhouette of a person who appeared to be looking out of the window. The hairs on the back of my neck stood up and I nearly shit myself. When you work nights, you think you have seen someone or something as you drive around and it often turns out to be a lamppost or a trick of the light. I stopped in my tracks and looked up slowly at the window again. It was still there, the clear outline of a person, stationary, looking out but strangely I could not make out any facial features so I knew it was not an actual person just a dense black shape. It is important to state here that if I thought someone had broken

34

into the nick then I would have obviously taken a dii course of action.

I ran back to the car, jumped in and drove off. Wl . returned to the nick an hour or so later, my colleagues were back inside and there was nothing visible in the window although the lighting conditions were exactly the same. From that moment on, I decided never to look up at the windows again whenever I came back in so that it would not interfere with my work.

There are plenty of people who have heard strange noises and doors slamming at Aldridge and I am sure there are plenty of other people who have not experienced anything at all, but there was another incident about a year later when a few of us were again on a night shift. The intention was for me to go into the disused cell block and play a joke on a student officer who was also in the building. If my mate could persuade him to go into the cells and it ended up with me jumping out from my hiding place and scaring him, it would be the perfect scenario. It would have been both character building and a team bonding exercise all in one.

I went into the cell block and walked into the cell opposite the charge desk. Once inside the cell, I felt a very strange pressure in my head and the temperature in the cell suddenly went ice cold. It will come as no surprise that I yet again nearly shit myself and as I walked out I felt a presence, as if someone was behind me.

As I have already said, there are plenty of people who have worked at Aldridge who will think this is crazy but maybe it is the case that some people are just more sensitive to these things than others. To expand on this point, while I was growing up I lived for a while with my family in an old house in Shropshire. There were plenty of times when I felt a strong presence, not particularly evil, just not that pleasant either. There were often footsteps in the middle of the night and sudden drops in temperature on numerous occasions. It was only when we moved out that my parents told me that they had both seen a female figure in a robe, only visible from the knees up, glide across the landing. The figure looked directly at them before walking through the wall. I am really glad they didn't tell me at the time.

Tipton Police Station, West Midlands

I had recently moved to the Operational Support Unit and was stationed at Tipton police station in Lower Church Lane. Next door was a disused church, and handily for everyone who worked there, a good pub opposite. There was not a front office open for the public or a 24/7 response team working from the nick and it was not used for anything other than housing the OSU and a surveillance team. It was an old building, which has since been knocked down and a modern one built on the same site to replace it.

This particular day was a Sunday morning and my serial had been posted to work on the Black Country derby between Wolverhampton Wanderers and West Bromwich Albion. If I recall rightly, I think it was an early kick off at 1230 so we would book on at 0800, get fed and then go off to the briefing.

I had not been on the department long and was really looking forward to working this game as there would be a big crowd and plenty to do. I decided to go in to Tipton early and press my uniform. There was an expectation on the OSU that high standards of appearance were maintained, irrespective of our duty, which on that day would be dealing with any disorder and monitoring the supporters who presented the most risk.

I drove to work and must have arrived at the nick at about 0630. The place was in darkness and I let myself in via the coded door lock. Once inside, I went upstairs to the crew rooms. It was a very old building and the staircase was wooden so you could always hear when people were coming and going.

I went into the kitchen area and was making a cup of tea when I heard the distinctive sound of someone coming up the stairs. I was quite surprised that someone else had decided to come in early so I shouted out, ' Do you fancy a brew?'

There was no reply so just thought to myself it must be an ignorant bastard, or more charitably, perhaps they didn't hear me. I went out of the kitchen and had a good look in all the crew rooms but there was no one else around.

I was ironing my shirt when I again heard the loud sound of someone coming up the stairs and there was no way it could have been anything else because the noise was so familiar to anyone who worked there. There was a rhythm to the footsteps and short time later I heard them again. I went and looked in every room on the floor and discovered that I was alone. At this point I started feeling very uneasy and went downstairs.

I looked everywhere in the nick. I was certain it was not a prank as no one knew I was coming in that early and my car was the only one on the car park when I had arrived. My feelings of unease had by now increased considerably, to the extent that I picked up my keys and went and sat in my car waiting for someone else to arrive, before going back into the nick with them. I pretended that I had just arrived a few seconds before my colleague and didn't mention what had happened. I also didn't bother going in that early ever again.

Lloyd House, Birmingham

Lloyd House had been built between 1960 and 1961 to be the headquarters for steel stockholders Stewarts and Lloyds Ltd. The first officers from the City of Birmingham Police moved into the building in the early part of 1973. However the move was not a welcome one, with staff complaining about poor heating conditions on some floors and the 'lack of character' of the building. It was still the same forty years later when I worked there as a Crown Court Liaison Officer.

One evening, I was in the office working late although bearing in mind any time past 1600 is classed as working late in headquarters. It was about 1730 and there were some urgent papers to get ready for court the following day, so I had stayed on to sort everything out and prepare the required amount of copies.

I sat at my desk working away with my head down when suddenly I caught a very strong whiff of tobacco and although alone in the office, I didn't think too much of it but it was definitely tobacco. Smoking was not allowed in the building and no one who worked in our department was a smoker.

I went to a small room at the end of the office where the photocopier was kept. The smell of tobacco was now even stronger. I saw a former colleague leaning out of the partially open window having a crafty fag. I saw him clearly but only from the waist upwards. There was nothing obscuring the view, his legs were just not there. I instinctively called out his name, and as I did so, he turned towards me and disappeared.

The crafty smoker was a retired copper who was always sneaking off for a cigarette, given half the chance, before he unfortunately passed away a year earlier. I remembered that he had been caught smoking in the photocopying room and blowing it out of the window quite a few times.

This was not scary in the slightest and was simple for me to work out. I had just seen the ghostly apparition of an old colleague.

Erith Police Station

After the pubs had closed around 11.30, no one ever came into the station so you were there alone. All other officers worked from the main station; the front office was only kept open to reassure the public, who never actually came in but they would phone if they needed police. I knew that each night was going to seem very long and lonely. If the other officers on the relief had time, I would get the occasional visitor to join me for a cup of tea and a chat, but that was it.

Erith is a district in the London borough of Bexley and the station was a typical Victorian police station, built around 1909. The design was such that when sitting in the front office you couldn't see the rear yard but you could always hear vehicles entering. It wasn't possible to see anyone approaching the front office either, until they had walked across the yard, into the charge room and then finally through to the front office. Police officers calling in had the option of going up some stairs to the parade room before entering the front office.

One night at about 2.30am, I heard someone walking across the floor of the upstairs parade room; I thought this strange as I had not heard a car enter the rear yard. However, I did have the radio on so thought nothing of it. I was sure that they would be checking their paperwork trays and that they would soon be down for a cup of tea. Strangely, I did not hear them come down and they did not appear. I also didn't hear any car leave the rear yard.

The following night at about the same time, the exact same thing happened and I was now becoming suspicious. A couple of nights later the same thing happened again, no car was heard but I heard the distinct sound of footsteps upstairs. As I was there for the week, I had hatched a plan to apprehend the apparent trespasser the moment I next heard their footsteps.

A few nights later I heard the footsteps and shot out of my chair, ran across the front office and was halfway up the stairs before the footsteps had fully crossed the room. I flew into the parade room and was surprised to find it empty. There were a couple of other rooms on the floor, which I searched but couldn't find anyone. The staircase is the only way down; by being up there I would have seen or heard anyone using it. I didn't mention it to my colleagues because, as you know, police officers do not need very much - if any - encouragement to mercilessly ridicule each other for the slightest thing.

A few months later I again found myself as station officer at Erith during the night duty. The same thing happened again a couple of times during the week. I went sprinting to the parade room and tried to apprehend the trespasser but again to no avail. Sometime later, I mentioned it to one of the older officers who said, "Oh, didn't you know that would have been the old Superintendent". He went on to explain that many years ago, the upstairs rooms were used as the Superintendent's flat, and he had some issues in his private life or something and the job were less than sympathetic, so he hanged himself from the rafters. The officer reckoned that the superintendent could often be heard at night walking around in what were his old rooms. I know that this officer could have been winding me up, but I know some of the other station officers have heard the footsteps and were also reluctant to mention it. At the time I didn't particularly believe in ghosts and had an open mind. I still do, but it does make you wonder. The station has since been sold off and turned into private flats, so whoever has got the upstairs flat might find that they have a sitting tenant.

Walsall Police Station

About ten years ago I was working as a custody assistant at Walsall Police station. The nick is a five story square block built in the mid 1960s, situated on the edge of the town centre. Now and then, I had the occasional burst of enthusiasm to lose some weight and get myself fitter. Luckily for me, the nick had a gym. It was a full-sized gym which could be used as a badminton court or for playing basketball. At one end there was a recess where there were some free weights and exercise machines.

I was on a night shift and it was not too busy for a change, with only a few prisoners in custody. The sergeant had no objection to me having a break. I went up to the changing rooms, which were off the corridor just outside the main gym doors. I got changed into my kit and switched on the lights before starting my routine. I always started on the rowing machine and I usually listened to the radio but for some reason, on this occasion, I didn't bother.

I began rowing away and getting into a rhythm but I soon felt very uncomfortable. I had not experienced this feeling before but it I felt like I was being watched. I had been in the gym on numerous occasions and had always felt fine.

I carried on rowing but the feeling would not go away, so much so that I went and checked that the fire exit door was closed and I had a look in the area where the mats for self-defence training where kept, to make sure that there was no-one hiding there. I really thought I was losing the plot and I had to convince myself that I was alone and there was no-one else in the gym. I walked back to the rowing machine but the feelings became more and more intense, and it felt as if someone was standing right behind me staring at the back of my head. I kept turning round but there was nothing behind me.

I decided to knock it on the head and go and have a shower. I switched off the lights and as I left the gym I heard an androgynous voice directly behind me say 'bye-bye'. Not 'good-bye' but a definite 'bye-bye'. I thought this was fucking bizarre and I was really trying to work out what on earth was going on.

I went into the changing rooms and had a very quick shower. There were three showers in total and they all had a push button system, which was on timer so after a few minutes the water would cut off and you would have to press the button again.

As was getting dressed I heard the sound of the shower start up. I got up and walked to the cubicles and saw that all three showers were now in full flow. I hastily grabbed my kit and stuffed it into my sports bag as I wanted to get the fuck out of there. As I stepped into the corridor it felt really cold. It was winter and it was a cold place due to the poor glazing but there was a distinct difference in temperature from when I had gone in a few minutes earlier, so much so that I could now see my own breath. There was also a really strong smell of old fashioned perfume, the kind your grandmother would wear. I ran as fast as I possibly could back to the block and I did not use the gym on nights ever again.

Authors note

Walsall Police Station closed in October 2016 and the building is now up for sale.

Bishopsgate Police Station, City of London

The City of London Police Hospital opened in June 1866. It was located behind the Bishopsgate Police Station. Police officers who had reported sick and were likely to be absent from duty for more than a few days were obliged to attend the Hospital for assessment. The Hospital also treated those who had been injured in the line of duty. On admission, they all received free medical and nursing care.

In 1936 the building was demolished and new Police Station opened in April 1939. The Hospital was located on the top floor of the building, which also contained accommodation for single and married policemen, and there was a rifle and revolver range in the basement. It remained in use a hospital until the introduction of the National Health Service. It is an impressive looking building in the heart of London

In the 1980s one of my friends was a detective constable and she shared a flat above Bishopsgate police station with two other officers from the City of London police. The flat had three bedrooms, a bathroom, living room and a kitchen. I was working for the British Transport Police based in Manchester and I was looking forward to going to visit my friend and stay overnight in London, as the flat is in a great location. For the purpose of this story I will refer to her as Joanne.

The first time I visited Joanne, I arrived quite late and after a long day and all the travelling I was feeling pretty tired. I went to bed in the middle of the three rooms and it wasn't long before I was fast asleep. During the night, I was woken up abruptly and I was unable to move my arms and legs. It felt like the bedding around me had been tucked in over tight. It was alarming at the time but as the feeling subsided, I drifted back to sleep. I woke up the next morning and brushed it off by telling myself it must have been a dream.

Sometime later I was again visiting Joanne, with another female colleague from Manchester and on this occasion it was our intention to stay for two nights. Our plans for the evening were scuppered though when Joanne was called out to an emergency incident and said that she wouldn't be back until the morning.

That left the two of us on our own in the flat, and when it came time for us to go to bed, my friend went to sleep in the room that I had stayed in previously and I slept in the room next door. I lay in bed and was just drifting off to sleep when I saw a woman standing at the door wearing a long grey dress with a lace collar. Now I was fully alert, I saw that her hair was in a bob and she wore gold rimmed glasses. She moved towards the bed and overcome with fear I instinctively hid under the blankets and I then felt them being pulled as I hung on with all my might before the 'tug of war' suddenly stopped. I tentatively peered from beneath the bedding to realise the woman was no longer in the room. Probably due to the sheer fear I had experienced, I did not move out of the bed and at some point I must have fallen asleep. I was woken up by Joanne coming home from her call-out the following morning.

As we sat together talking, it was commented upon by Joanne how rough I looked. I told her what had happened and she just laughed it off saying it must have been due the amount we had to drink before going to bed, but when my other friend got up she told us that she had experienced an incident identical to mine, on my previous visit when I had slept in the same room. She had also discovered that all the coat hangers that had been on the door when she went to sleep were now in the waste paper basket. I knew that we hadn't drunk anywhere near enough to have both been imagining things like this.

We decided to only stay the one night and after breakfast we caught the train back to Manchester and later found out through a mutual friend that Joanne had been experiencing unusual goings on in the flat for some time and was looking to move. Joanne did move out shortly after our visit but she clearly hadn't wanted to discuss it as she had not said anything to me.

A few months later I was chatting to a PC who used to work in the City of London and he knew Bishopsgate well. I told him I had stayed there and without any prompting from me, he asked if I had met the ghost who lived there. I naturally recounted the incidents and he told me that the hospital was bombed during WW II and the matron was killed. He reckoned that the ghost was the matron doing her rounds, and after my experiences, I think he is probably right.

Authors note

During my research, I contacted a police officer from the City of London, who had posted a picture of Bishopsgate on his twitter feed. I asked whether he had any information regarding similar incidents and he kindly provided the following background information.

'The ghost is reckoned to be that of Evelyn Rolfe, a nurse at the hospital. She had worked for the City Police for some while as she can be found in 1911, nursing a couple of the men involved in the Houndsditch Murders. Evelyn was badly injured when Bishopsgate Police Station was bombed in September 1940 and subsequently died.

A colleague was training late one evening, on the 6th or 7th floor of Bishopsgate where the hospital was situated. The officer said she was alone after the training had finished, and the door to the room slowly opened and then closed. She went out of the room, but there was no-one there. She called out that she knew it was Nurse Rolfe and that she wasn't afraid of her. The City of London Roll of Honour records the following-P/Nurse Evelyn Rolfe S.R.N. Died 9 September 1940 aged 65. Fatally injured by enemy action at the City of London Police Hospital.'

Sparkhill Police Station, Birmingham
Now I will start by saying that I am not a big believer in ghosts, however I can recall several occasions during the mid 1980s when as a probationary constable I would be posted to cover the front office on nights at Sparkhill Police Station, which is an old building on the Stratford Road in Birmingham. It is now home to the West Midlands Police Museum.

I sometimes heard footsteps and what sounded like furniture being moved about upstairs in the CID office. At the time that these incidents occurred there was no doubt that I was the only person in the building. I would often have a walk around, checking the security and stretching my legs. No one else could come into the station without me knowing.

Whenever I heard the noises, I would go upstairs and investigate. As I entered, the whole room would feel unusually cold, even during the summer months. I found it very unusual that there would also be a faint floral smell, and this in the days when CID offices tended to stink of stale tobacco as smoking was still allowed inside the building. There was of course no-one there and I was subsequently told that there were other police officers that had experienced similar incidents to mine.

Cottesloe Police Station, Western Australia

Cottesloe Police Station was originally opened in 1908 during the Gold Rush era, which is considered to be very old in Western Australia. The police station today comprises of two old buildings separated by a modern portacabin in between them.

I would describe the buildings as two detached single storey buildings and they are situated next the Fremantle rail line on Curtin Avenue (named after former Prime Minister John Curtin). The most northerly building is now the front office with the one and only cell and interview room. The portable cabin was, at the time I was there, the main police office for report writing. The southernmost building was the dining area, lockers, armoury and toilets.

Towards the end of 2014, I was serving as a sergeant on a newly formed local policing team covering the southern part of the Cottesloe sub-district. I was on an afternoon shift which was a 1400 to midnight and I was on duty with two other officers, a female probationer called Sarah, and 'Hilly', a senior constable with thirty years service.

At about 2200 hours we were all in the station. I was speaking to my two colleagues about an incident earlier in the day and after our conversation, they went back out and resumed their mobile patrol. I remained in the station because just like my time as a sergeant in Wolverhampton, there was a mountain of paperwork and incident reports for me to look at.

The front building was locked up and alarmed and this is the only other entrance to the police station other than the electric sliding gate at the front, which leads to the car park that runs alongside the railway line. A swipe card system was used to open the gate and they were only issued to officers at the station.

into the enquiry counter and looked after any prisoners that were brought in. It was light years away from the modern custody blocks and the role that the custody sergeant carries out today. Canterbury Road only had three or four cells but was still used for processing people who had been arrested. The building dates back to 1904.

I was working a night shift and had taken over with no prisoners in the cells. It was a pretty routine night for the first couple of hours until not long after midnight when I was in the station on my own. I was checking the lost property book when I heard a cell door slam shut. It made me jump and has a very distinctive sound that most people who have worked in cell block will testify.

The office is quite small and the only way to the cells is through a door that runs directly from the office. Although I was certain that no one could have entered the cells without me knowing, my mind tried to rationalise it by telling me that one of the troops must have brought in a prisoner. I walked the few yards to the door hoping to see an officer who was going to tell me about his arrest.

There was nobody there and even more bizarrely all the cell doors were wide open. I could not work it out and you think 'what the fuck has just happened?' because it doesn't make any sense.

(2) In 1988 I was working on the D Division, based at Queens Road nick in Aston. There were also two other stations on the sub division at Nechells Green and Canterbury Road in Perry Barr, which in those days were both kept open 24/7.

One set of nights I had to cover the office at Canterbury Road. In the daytime there were plenty of people about as the Scenes of Crime department and a surveillance team had their offices in the building. There had been plenty of stories about the place being haunted and rumours of sightings of a bobby in an old style uniform being seen in the station and in the back yard. I was well aware of the stories but not concerned in the slightest. I was more frightened in those days of one of the sergeants finding an old accident book festering in my locker.

It had been an uneventful night, about the third one in a set of seven that we used to work in those days and I was sitting at the desk reading a book. The desk was facing the public enquiry counter so I could see whoever came into the nick and they would be able see me. Directly to my right was a doorway leading to the cells that were only a few feet away. No-one could possibly enter the cell area without walking past me.

There had only been a few visitors who had come to produce their driving documents and it was about 1am and I was wide awake, and to be honest, feeling a bit bored. Suddenly, I heard the unmistakable loud clang of a cell door being slammed shut. The metal on metal sound carried on ringing out for a few seconds but to me it seemed much longer. It felt like it was shuddering through my whole body. You have to bear in mind the cells were a very short distance from where I was sitting, and where I remained sitting, unable to move through sheer fear. I have never felt that frightened before and I never felt anything like that fear in the rest of my career either. Even during my short time in the job, I had faced some dangerous situations, which had got my arse twitching but this was something completely different. It was a different kind of fear.

I tried to work out what had happened and I tried to explain it to myself. I wished it was a joke, a gust of wind or a dodgy radiator but it was none of these things - it was a cell door being slammed shut a few feet behind me - yet I knew that there was no-one there. It felt like I was frozen to the spot.

My senses were now heightened and I nearly jumped out of the chair when the phone eventually rang. It was the duty controller asking if I wanted to be brought back to Queens

Road for a refreshment break. The controller must have sensed something in my voice because he asked me if I was okay. I told him what had happened and he offered to send a panda to me, but I suppose a bit of bravado kicked in and I told him I was fine.

I put the phone down and walked into the cell corridor. There were only four cells and one was full of old phone equipment. The other cells were empty and all the doors were wide open.

I got through the rest of the week without incident. The following night a puppy was handed in and I kept it in the office with me, which helped to take my mind of things. Not long after this incident, I passed my driving course and was never posted to Canterbury Road office again. After what had happened, that suited me just fine.

Hindley, Greater Manchester

Hindley is a town a few miles from Wigan and is covered by the Greater Manchester Police. The old police station situated on Castle Hill Road closed in 2007 and is now a dental surgery. In 2004 the station was not fully operational and very few police officers actually worked inside so there were long periods of time when the station was empty. It is an impressive old building.

Around this time I was assigned to carry out some partnership work with an Education Welfare Officer, concentrating on young people who were playing truant from school. The woman I was working with was professional and pleasant company so everything was going well as we patrolled the locality together, with me driving a police van.

When lunchtime arrived, we went to Hindley police station so we could sit down and have break. There was no one else in the station and I directed the EWO along the corridor to the refreshment area.

A short time later, I went to join her and found her looking very upset and shocked. She told me that there was something in the building and wanted to leave. I was obviously concerned and checked the all the offices and rooms but there was no one else in the nick. The EWO insisted that she wanted to leave the building immediately, which we did and parked up a short distance away.

I was worried about what was wrong as she was clearly upset. She then told me that she had seen a figure in the corridor with its back towards her. It was a male wearing a black cape and he had black hair but it was not a person in solid physical form. She looked away for a second and the figure had vanished. There was no doubt in her mind that she had seen a ghost and no doubt in mine that she had experienced a traumatic incident. What was also certain was the fact that she would not enter the building under any circumstances again.

I have met the same EWO several times over the years and she is adamant that what she saw on that day in Hindley really was a ghost.

Four:
Various Locations

Llanrhos Church, North Wales

In August 1939 my parents married at a small old church in Llanrhos about a mile and a half outside Llandudno, North Wales. Twenty or so years later, I drove past the same church late one evening as I was making my way home. I was alone in my car and I turned off the main road into a small, well used lane just as it began to rain. Ahead of me was a left hand bend where my headlights lit up a stationary figure standing at the side of the road. I could not work out whether it was a male or female because the person was wearing a duffel coat, or something similar, and had pulled the hood up, I assumed because of the sudden downpour. I dipped my headlights as I approached and pulled up alongside with the intention of offering the person a lift. After stopping, I straight-away opened my window ready to invite the person into my car, only to find myself alone; there was no sign at all of anybody at the scene nor anywhere nearby. It goes without saying that the apparition was sufficiently 'real' to cause me, without hesitation, to stop in order to offer the person a lift and shelter from the rain.

Many years later, the road bend where this incident took place was modified in the interests of safety and an express-way now dissects the lane nearby. Some people who live locally may know that an ancient footpath leads from the church and across the lane, en-route to a manor house, which is now a hotel situated in nearby woods. Further on, still within the wooded area, it is possible to pass via stone steps, down the hillside towards Conwy where, long ago, access to the weekly market was by ferry boat. The pathway and the stone steps are known locally as, 'The Monks Walk'.

I have obviously thought a great deal about that evening over the years and in 2015 I had a letter published in the magazine of the National Association of Retired Police Officers (NARPO). I told my story and concluded by saying that I would be interested to hear from anyone who, knowing the area, feels that they too saw or sensed 'a presence' at or near the spot on a particular occasion.

Sometime later, NARPO forwarded a letter to me from a retired police officer who lived in Cheshire. The letter explained how the same thing had happened to his father in the 1930s. The officer's father used to walk on the footpaths and fields in the area as he was courting a girl from Deganwy, who he later married and became the officer's mother. The letter detailed how his father had also seen a hooded figure near to the same spot.

His father had walked past Llanrhos church and seen a hooded figure just standing there, and straight after he had passed, he turned around for a second look but the person had disappeared. The retired officer often thought about the story, and that his dad had obviously thought it was a ghost. Apparently, monks in the area had carried many large stones to supply the masons who were building Llanrhos church.

Bromford, Birmingham

In the mid 1960s I moved into a police house in Hillcross Walk, which was on the Bromford Estate in Birmingham. I had moved in with my husband and my two young children, a daughter aged four and our two year old son. My husband was a police constable stationed at Duke St, just outside the city centre, where he worked as a police motorcyclist. The house was bigger than the flat we had just moved from and with two young children the extra space was most welcome. It was a three bedroom, semi-detached house among a block of four police houses.

Not long after we had moved in we were visited by two friends of ours, Mike and Janet. It was the first time that they had come to our new home and after I had put the kids to bed Janet and I settled down in the lounge while the men went out for a drink at a nearby pub. Janet was a very level headed person but she immediately seemed nervous and sat with a cushion on her lap, as if she was trying to protect herself. Janet told me that she did not feel comfortable in the house.

A short time later, we heard the front door open and someone go running upstairs. I presumed it was my husband who must have forgotten something and I expected him to pop his head round the door. Janet and I both heard all the doors upstairs open and slam shut one by one, before hearing the sound of someone running back down the stairs and out of the front door. I looked out the window but I could not see anyone walking away from the house.

It all seemed very strange and I was livid. I assumed it must have been my husband because I could not think of anything else. This had certainly not helped with how uneasy Janet was feeling, so much so that when she wanted to go to the toilet, she insisted that I went upstairs with her and sat on the landing.

When Alan and Mike returned I took them to task for what I assumed was a prank. In turn they were angry with me at the suggestion and insisted they had done no such thing, so much so that things became a little heated. I could tell from their reaction that they were telling the truth so whatever had happened was very concerning and not long after this incident there were further strange occurrences in the house.

One of my favourite pieces of furniture was a glass display cabinet. It was kept locked and the key was kept separately in a draw. On numerous occasions I would be dusting or would just happen to look in the cabinet to find that an ornament had been turned around and was facing the wrong way. It was always the same piece, a porcelain Grecian woman. No other pieces were ever touched and I always kept the cabinet locked. I would turn it back and even placed it on a mat as someone suggested it was caused by vibrations although no other piece ever moved. The mat did not stop it from moving anyway because it would frequently be found by me, or my husband, facing the wrong way. As you can imagine, it was all very unnerving. It was a precise movement of the ornament, always facing the opposite direction it should be.

Janet visited on one more occasion and she told me she would not come back because of the way the house made her feel. We remained in the house for a further eighteen months but it was never a happy home. There always seemed to be some sort of sickness or illness in the house. I was glad to leave as every time I found the ornament had moved, I felt more and more uncomfortable.

The same cabinet and ornament have since moved with us to several different homes and never once since leaving that house has the same thing happened. I was later told that no-one ever stopped in the house for very long, which came as no surprise to me.

RAF Cosford, Shropshire

Royal Air Force Station Cosford, or RAF Cosford for short, is situated in Shropshire, just to the North West of Wolverhampton and next to the village of Albrighton. Public Order courses are hosted here utilising a converted aircraft hangar on the site. The facilities allow officers to experience and train for a variety of public order situations, and tactics for policing major events are also taught at the site. I worked there as a trainer for a few years until my retirement from the police in 2011.

There were always tales of the 'haunted' hangars and there has been activity reported in other hangars, in particular one that houses an old Lincoln RF398 long range heavy bomber built in 1945. She is the last of the piston-engined bombers used by the RAF and apparently is frequently visited by the ghost of a young man although the hangar that we used for our training is situated some distance away from that one.

One morning, together with some other training staff, I was taking a Taser class on the temporary range that we had set up. The lesson we were delivering to the students was the procedures for loading and firing. One of officers in the group was having some problems and was struggling to grasp this part of the lesson. I took her from away from the group to a quieter area for some one-to-one tuition. This was standard practice if a student needed a bit more help. I put her at ease to take some of the pressure off and we then resumed training in our own little corner.

As we continued to work through the procedures, I was directly facing the student, standing an arms length away from her. Without any warning, there was a sudden movement of her head, which I would describe as a twitch or a jerk and she cried out as if receiving some sort of short sharp pain.

I asked her what had happened and she responded by wanting to know if I had just tugged her hair. I pointed out the obvious fact that I was standing directly in front of her and she would have seen me if I had done it. The student was emphatic that someone, who must have been standing close to her, had just pulled her hair. This was weird because I had just seen her head move as if that was the case.

We were both confused but somehow we managed to laugh it off and carry on with the lesson. I am convinced that the student thought that another trainer had crept up on her but I know for a fact that they didn't and there was no one else standing within 20-30 metres of us when this incident happened.

On another occasion in the same hangar, I was working with a colleague on a Taser scenario. The officer I was working with was someone who I would describe as a solid, reliable officer. I knew him as the kind of person that you would want alongside you in a difficult situation. He was not someone that would ever play jokes or piss about at work. Just for the purpose of this story, I will refer to him as Jeff.

The training department had been given an old double decker bus, which we were using in this particular scenario. It was a great asset as it provided a realistic environment for some of the challenges that officers would face out on the streets. The scenario involved an instructor on the bus, suitably dressed in protective gear, acting as the aggressor or suspect. The instructor would often be waiting alone on the bus for considerable periods of time whilst students were briefed before they were brought into the hangar. My role in the training exercise was to be the designated safety officer, with a responsibility for taking an overview of the action and intervening if it was appropriate. Jeff was waiting on the bus.

I saw the students being brought into the hangar to start the exercise so it was a good time to check that Jeff, who had been on the bus waiting a fair while, was okay and ready to start. Jeff was sitting on the top-deck back-seat and confirmed over the radio that he was fine.

I apologised to him for the delay, as the briefing had gone on longer than usual but Jeff told me it was no problem as he had been talking to the ghost who was sitting alongside him. He even asked if I could see him, which from my position I couldn't. I have absolutely no doubt, from his tone of voice and knowing his character, that this question was being asked in all seriousness as Jeff spoke to me in a very matter of fact way. I didn't think about it too deeply at the time, probably because the scenario then started and it was completed without any problems.

The next day, I was sitting with Jeff in the instructors' room and the conversation turned to the scenario on the bus, specifically about what he had said to me the day before over the radio. Jeff, very calmly, told me that he had gone home after work and told his wife about what he had experienced on the bus. During the conversation she didn't seem surprised at all and she asked Jeff if the ghost was a black teenage boy wearing a bandana. Jeff confirmed that indeed it was and asked how she knew. His wife told him, 'you've brought him home with you and he's standing next to you' and as she said this, the boy disappeared.

I was genuinely astounded, as I think anyone would be, but at no point did I not believe what Jeff was telling me.

The Bull Ring Shopping Centre, Birmingham

I worked as a security guard in the Bull Ring shopping centre in Birmingham. At this time I was also a Special Constable. This was before all the recent redevelopment but even then it was still a vast area. When all the shops closed, there would be a loudspeaker announcement telling members of the public that the centre was closing. The security guards on duty would then conduct a physical sweep of the centre to make sure that nobody was locked in.

The shops had their own individual alarm systems and the centre had its own movement sensors, which would activate in the security control room. There was CCTV covering the centre, which was also monitored in the control room. I was working nights with two colleagues when the movement sensor alarms kept going off. We would then go and make a physical check of the area and it was established that the sensors were working fine in tracking our movements.

As soon as we had left the area, the activations would start up again. Between the three of us, we could not work it out because there was nothing visible causing them to activate and there was clearly no fault with the system.

Later on in the shift, a local beat bobby from Digbeth turned up for a cup of tea. We hadn't called the police about what was happening but we had a good working relationship with the local officers so this impromptu visit was not unusual. We explained to the officer what was happening and he also thought it was strange so he requested a dog handler for a more thorough search to take place. This would not be an option today with all the cuts to police resources but in those days each area usually had at least one dog handler duty.

The dog handler arrived and we explained to him the problems we were experiencing. As a group, we all went to the part of the shopping centre where the activations were taking place and we followed the enthusiastic dog and handler to the top of a switched off escalator.

The dog handler had told us he was going to let the dog, a German Shepherd, off the lead and to wait where we were standing, on the escalator. There was no audible alarm in the actual area where we were experiencing all the problems; the sound was activated in the control room only.

At the top of the stairs the dog, who had been eager for a run, stopped dead in his tracks. The dog's hackles were raised and he began barking and growling ferociously. The dog was clearly disturbed by something and would not respond to the handler telling him to move. Even when he tried to push him, the dog would not move. It was an experienced, well trained dog and the handler said that the dog had never behaved like this before. Nothing could make the dog move into the area so we had to make do with our own efforts.

There was no fault ever found on the alarm and no evidence from the CCTV of anyone being in the area but something had been causing the sensors to go off and something none of us could see had clearly upset the dog.

On another occasion, I was walking the through the centre after everywhere was closed, conducting a final sweep. All the exits and doors were secure and everywhere was empty. I looked across to some tables outside Gino's restaurant and I was surprised to see a man sitting outside, slumped over one of the tables, completely still. It was strange that he had not been seen before and the only thing I could think of was that it might be one of the homeless people who must have been hiding in the toilets. They would spend as much time in the shopping centre as they could, trying to keep warm but they were never any problem when we asked them to leave.

I radioed the control room and asked them to put a camera on him until I finished my checks. My colleague in the control room confirmed that he could see the man and said that he would keep an eye on him. It was my intention to wake the man up and let him out after I had completed what I was doing.

A short time later I went back to Gino's but the man had gone. My colleague in the control room said one minute he was there but when he looked again, he had vanished. I can categorically say that there was no way out of the area without me physically unlocking the door to let him out. The man had simply disappeared into thin air.

I was not the only person to have experienced strange goings on in the shopping centre. Another security guard was thrown forcibly into the back of a service lift by something that could not be seen. An invisible presence picked him up and threw him like a rag doll. He refused to work in that area ever again.

A private house in Staffordshire

What I am about to tell you took place while I was off duty and in my own home. I've always had an open mind regarding the afterlife however this incident has made me reappraise my beliefs. One morning in March 2016, I was sitting in my lounge watching television. As I looked at the screen, I witnessed a vapour like swirling mist forming in front of it. It was so thick that it began distorting the TV image, so much so that I could no longer see what was on the screen at all. It remained swirling in front of me for about for about 20 seconds, before drifting slowly off and disappearing out of sight completely. I will point out here that there was no-one in the house who was having a crafty fag, and there were no faults with the TV that could have been responsible for what I had just seen.

As soon as the incident had ended, I went and spoke to my friend who was staying with me at the time and told them what had just taken place. I believed that something involving a death was going to happen that day. It was a very definite, strong feeling but something that is also difficult to put into words.

Later that same day, I received a text telling me that an old friend, and former police officer, had been found dead in unfortunate and upsetting circumstances.

Former police house, Sutton Coldfield

Around the year 2000, I worked as a police staff member at Sutton Coldfield Police Station, Birmingham. At the rear of the main police station building on Anchorage Road, there are a few old police houses, which at that time were being used as offices by various departments. I was working in an admin role in one of the houses. I don't know who had lived in the house before or when they were built but the main station was opened in 1960.

As I lived locally, I often used to arrive early and be the only person in the building. One morning this was again the case and I made myself a drink and settled down to start work. After a short time, I needed to copy some documents and went to the photocopier, which was situated under the stairs. I had been standing there for a few minutes when I felt a sharp painful kick to the back of my left knee which caused my leg to buckle. I was taken by surprise and immediately turned around, after recovering my balance, to see that there was no one there. I was still the only person in the building and no one could have possibly kicked me and run off without me seeing them.

It was not a muscle spasm or anything like that, but a definite blow to the back of my leg and it made me feel very unsettled. I was glad when my other colleagues started to arrive and I was no longer alone.

The Converted Farm, West Midlands

I bought a house in 1997 situated in open countryside to the north of Birmingham. In estate agent style, I would describe it as a development that was converted from barn and farm buildings, a lovely location just the right distance away from the built up area and amenities, quaint, full of character and very peaceful, gated entrance, excellent conversion. There were twelve mews type houses around a landscaped courtyard.

I have served in both the Royal Military Police and West Midlands Police and there is a strong police connection to the property as the estate it stands on was sold to Sir Robert Peel, who had all the buildings demolished in 1817, apart from the stable block and farm buildings. The main house that the farm served had stood since 1300. The surviving farm buildings, after lying in disrepair for some time, were developed into homes in the early 1990s. Nearby, there have been extensive archaeological surveys, which revealed evidence of Bronze

Age burnt mounds which may have been burial grounds around 3000 ago.

In 1829, Sir Robert decided to reorganise the way that London was policed and as a result of his reform, the new Metropolitan Police force was born. In some ways, I suppose I should have been grateful to him for not knocking down what was to be my new home.

I stayed at the house for about eighteen months and there were a number of incidents which took place that caused me a lot of concern at the time, and some twenty years later I still cannot fully understand. The incidents and overwhelming horrible feelings I endured were not constant but when they did happen, they made me question my own sanity.

Not long after I moved in, I began to feel that I was being watched. The feelings were really strong and began taking place when I was taking a shower and on one occasion it felt like someone was getting into bed alongside me. The feelings continued and more physical activity took place when a picture frame was found broken on the floor and I began hearing footsteps around my house. I decided to take action and went to see a priest at a nearby church. After telling him about what was taking place, he came round and blessed the house but if anything the situation worsened.

My cat, which was a clean, well behaved cat, began shitting everywhere and when I looked after a friend's perfectly healthy dog for a few weeks, it was constantly throwing up but was fine again when it went home. A visitor to my house once told me they felt as if someone was physically helping them when they went upstairs.

As time passed, I spoke to a few neighbours who also reported strange events including seeing the apparition of a nun. It made me realise how reluctant people are to speak about these things. I was glad to move out after eighteen months. I remember a sergeant, who grew up in the area, advising me not to move there because it was haunted. I think he was right.

Nottingham City Hospital

Working as a beat officer with responsibility for a large hospital complex requires that you have good working relationships with the permanent security team. You spend a lot of time in each other's company, discussing events that have taken place and exchanging information.

I'd never heard of 'orbs' before. I didn't know anything about them. You may not know anything about them either, as you read this. They are, as far as I understand and has been explained to me, the spirits of dead people. The 'orb' itself is a circle of light, like a ball, floating in the air and is usually best seen in photographs. You can see them in quite a few photographs. You may have some yourself but are so far unaware of them. Shaun, the security guard, told me about them. Shaun is a person who you would describe, if you met him, as a genuinely nice bloke. A thoroughly decent chap, always helpful, outgoing and positive, yet on occasions strangely diffident and reserved. He used to live in a small house in a street built on land which was once a mortuary, near the back of the hospital. He showed me numerous photographs of his family in their living room. There were orbs everywhere in these pictures. Large ones, small ones, groups of orbs together, on the walls and in the air, just floating.

One afternoon, we were discussing this phenomenon in the security office. Shaun had brought these photos into work for us to examine as evidence. Clearly they were there in the pictures. Nigel, a fellow guard and always the pragmatist, stated they were just dust particles either in the room at the time, and reflected at the moment the photo was taken, or specks on the lens. If that was the case then there was a lot of dust about! Would that explain other occasions when there were no orbs or dust in any photographs? Apparently the same camera had been used to take pictures in Shaun's new house, miles away from the hospital, where not a single orb had been found in any photographs. Not only this, a colleague of Shaun had borrowed his camera to take on holiday. No orbs have ever been revealed in any of those holiday snaps either. I'm afraid we had a laugh at Shaun's expense though, as Nigel made some photocopies of some of Shaun's photos and drew smiley faces in the orbs. But as always, I maintain an open mind about it. The orbs that is, not the smiley faces!

The new car park across from the back of the maternity building was once an old red brick nurses accommodation. It had been empty and boarded up for ten years or more. I was told it was one of the first of such old buildings to have been abandoned. It was Shaun who had told me this. He also told me that it was due to orbs and other paranormal phenomenon. In essence, the main reason the building was abandoned is that no one was willing to live in it any longer, it was so haunted. So many times, apparently, nurses had complained of wailing and moaning in the night. Footsteps along the dark corridors which stopped outside rooms, followed by tapping on the doors. There was never anyone there when these sounds were investigated.

On one occasion Shaun was asked to investigate an incident with a colleague long after all the residents had left. As in other similar calls, it was thought local kids had gained entry to the buildings by pulling up the boards from the windows but as they drew up in their van they could see that there did not appear to be anything insecure. In fact a cursory check around the outside revealed it to be completely intact and secure. Shaun unlocked the main door and walked in, torch in hand.

I would guess that walking into a building such as this, knowing its reputation as he did, Shaun was probably a little on edge to say the least. Undeterred, he stepped inside with his colleague, Tony, behind him. They walked along the corridor on the ground floor. It was a calm night with no wind so what happened next made them assume there were kids in the building after all. Ten yards ahead of them, a light bulb flew across the corridor from one empty room into another and smashed on the floor in the room ahead of them and to their left. They walked straight into the room where the bulb had come from and shone their torches around all four walls, fully expecting to see at least one giggling teenager. Nothing- no one there. The ceiling light was hanging there, swinging gently minus a bulb. A breeze then started, gentle at first but then inexplicably strong, swirling around the two men. It was icy cold despite the fact it was a warm night. At that moment both men state they heard someone whispering to them, not from a distance but right up close and directly in their ears. They were multiple layered voices in a hurried and peremptory tone, though they could not understand what was being said.

Shaun reached for his phone, not to make a call but to take a photograph. He has stated that he amazed himself at the level of composure it took him to do this as he fumbled in the torchlight to prepare his phone for camera mode. He took a single photograph of Tony standing there in the corridor in his yellow coat, at the doorway where the bulb had flown across their path. There are orbs everywhere in this photograph. They were behind Tony, over his shoulder and gathered around him in a group, as though curious and wanting to see and be seen.

I have seen this photo and Shaun's other photos. I've looked on the internet for orbs. Have a look yourself. You'll have to decide what you think about them. The building I have described no longer exists and it is now a very smart new car park. Before it was demolished, Shaun never ventured inside again.

Authors note

This account included with the kind permission of author Jonathan Nicholas, who is perhaps best known for his book 'Who'd be a copper? Thirty years a frontline British cop'. This story however, is taken from his other bestselling book 'Hospital Beat', which is an honest account of his ten years working at Nottingham City Hospital (although described as fiction to avoid disciplinary issues with his employers). Jonathan has informed me that this is a true account of his involvement in events at the hospital. Other paranormal incidents are also featured in the book.

Five:
Incidents Attended

Woolworths, Erdington High Street, Birmingham

In the winter of 1998, I was based at Erdington Police Station, Birmingham. Erdington is situated about four miles north of Birmingham city centre. The area is dominated by the High Street, a busy shopping area with shops, market areas and local businesses. It is famous for being the first suburb in Birmingham to be bombed in World War II, when on 9 August 1940, a German plane dropped eight bombs in the area resulting in the City's first fatality.

At some point during the day, some supposedly reliable information had been received that there was going to be a ram raid style burglary at a Woolworths 'somewhere' in the West Midlands area, although the information was not reliable enough to pinpoint the actual branch where this would take place. Ram-raiding is a variation on a burglary in which a stolen van or car, is driven through the windows or doors of a closed shop, usually a department store or jewellers shop, to allow the baddies to loot it. It was very popular at the time among the criminal fraternity, particularly in the run up to Christmas.

When I arrived at work for my night shift, I found out that I had drawn the short straw. I was told that a cunning and well thought out strategy had been put together, which involved posting two officers to sit in Woolworths and deal with whatever came crashing through the front doors. A female colleague and I had been chosen to spend the night in Woolies, and our safety was clearly paramount to senior officers, as the only instructions we were given consisted of advising us to keep well away from the front of the shop. This was disappointing, as I knew from visiting the store regularly to deal with shoplifters, that this was where the pic n' mix counter was located.

We got our kit together and walked over to Woolies, which was situated on the corner of the High Street and Barnabas Road. It only took a few minutes, if that, to walk over from the nick and meet the manager who was going to let us in. It had been arranged that we would come out of the shop at 0530 and meet with another member of staff and hand over to them.

The ground floor of the shop was the retail area. Leading off from this was an enclosed staircase which leads up to the staff canteen and toilets. It used to be a café but I think at this point in time it was just used by people that worked there. The manager showed us where everything was and we left our coats in the canteen area before settling down at the back of the shop after he had left us to it.

The duty was not as boring as I had anticipated, as we were nicely tucked away in the toy section and there was loads of stuff for us to mess about with to pass the time away. Throughout the night though, there were intermittent loud noises. They consisted of loud bangs and scraping noises, which I put down to it just being an old building or perhaps a generator. My colleague though was a bit more concerned and asked me to go up the stairs with her when she wanted to use the toilet.

The night soon passed and we put the toys away as the time for us to stand down from our mission soon arrived. We both went back up the stairs and collected our coats and started walking back down the stairs. My colleague was walking in front of me and as we reached about halfway, I heard a male voice say clearly and loudly 'Goodbye'. We both turned around immediately and looked up to the top of the stairs, which we could clearly see from our position. Standing at the top was a black solid mass that formed the shape of a large male, but it had nothing else to distinguish it. It was the silhouette of a person but I was close enough to see that it definitely was not an actual person.

Instinctively and without any conversation, we both clattered down the stairs and ran as fast as we could through the shop to the back door. I felt terrified - and my colleague certainly looked terrified. Outside the shop the guy we were meant to meet was waiting in his car. We told him we had finished for the night but we didn't mention anything else. As we walked back to the station it was clear from the conversation that we had both seen and heard the same thing. It had shaken us both up a lot.

Back at the nick, some other members of the shift were sitting in the office doing paperwork and we told them what had just happened. It will come as no surprise they didn't believe what they were told and just took the piss out of us. They probably thought we were joking.

To put this into context for anyone who may be thinking I am of a nervous disposition, I can assure you I am not. I am a former Royal Marine who has seen active service and I have boxed professionally. In a one-on-one situation I don't fear any man but this was definitely not a human and it was a genuinely frightening experience for us both.

Authors note

This particular Woolworths opened on 8th November 1930. It sadly closed in January 2009 and later reopened as a B & M store. On a recent visit to Erdington, I spoke with a member of staff who had worked there during its time as a Woolworths. She told me that over the years there had been several reports of items appearing to throw themselves off display stands and on one occasion during the daytime, the sighting of an apparition of a woman at the top of a stairway.

Betley Signal Box, near Crewe

In April 2011 I was working in the British Transport Police control room located in Birmingham. A call came through from the ambulance control room that they had received a call from a railway signal box in Betley, near Crewe. The ambulance control room said they did not know what the call was about because it disconnected. The signal box called another three times and a voice spoke only once saying, 'ambulance please'.

BTP control then phoned the signal box. The call was answered but no-one spoke and concern naturally grew as to whether or not someone really did need an ambulance. Calls were then made to network rail who said that the signal box had not been used for five years but they confirmed that ambulance control had passed the right number for the box.

A BTP controller made a further call and when the call was answered, the voice sounded strange. The male identified themselves as a signaller and the sound of a train could be heard in the background. The controller tried to confirm why an ambulance was needed with the male but the call disconnected.

In view of the confusion, police officers were sent to the scene to investigate. When they arrived they reported back that the signal box at Betley had been demolished some years earlier. All the control room staff on duty were left completely baffled by this incident.

Authors note

As a matter of interest, official railway records show that an accident happened at Betley Road on 17th November 1954 when a class 'D' freight train was travelling on the down slow line, at low speed in fog. The train ran past a light signal that was showing red at the entrance to a block section. The train then collided with the rear of another freight train. The engine of the class 'D' train was overturned the driver was fatally injured. The fireman and the guard on the leading train also received injuries and were taken to hospital by ambulance for treatment. (source www.railwayarchives.com)

Brierley Hill, West Midlands

In the summer of 1976 I was the duty inspector working nights at Brierley Hill. Brierley Hill is a small town in the Black Country forming part of the Dudley Metropolitan Borough. I had been out on patrol and at about midnight I returned to the station and walked into the front office.

I could see a young couple talking to a constable at the enquiry desk. As the constable saw me, he looked at me with an expression that suggested he needed some help and guidance. I went over to assist and the young couple explained that some sort of paranormal incident was taking place in their home. They believed that there was some sort of spirit in their young daughter's bedroom. As luck would have it, another constable then walked into the police station who was uncommitted, so I told the couple that we would both return with them to their home.

The house they lived in had been built on an area of land known locally as Rectory Fields and was a fairly modern semi-detached house. When we arrived the couple who lived next door were sitting in the lounge, looking after the four year old daughter of the couple who had come into the police station. The young girl was upstairs in bed and we went to her bedroom with her parents and we found that she was awake. The little girl was very calm and did not seem worried in any way. I spoke to the girl who confirmed that she was not frightened and it was then explained by her parents that whenever the girl went to leave the room, the spirit became restless.

I asked the girl to get out of bed and to go downstairs with her mother. As soon as she got out of bed, a frantic banging began in the corner of the room. It sounded like something was either the other side the wall or trapped in the wall itself. The

75

girl went downstairs and the banging became more frenzied getting louder and louder but there was nothing in the room that could have been the cause of the noise.

We all went downstairs and the banging continued. Together with the constable, we went next door with the neighbours to search their house. There was nothing and no-one that could be making the noise.

We returned to the house experiencing the problems and spoke with the parents and the little girl. We all went back upstairs and as the girl entered the bedroom the noise began to diminish and as she climbed into her bed the noise stopped completely. The girl was still not frightened in any way. As soon as she got out of bed, the banging started and got louder as we again left the room. I thought it would be a good idea for everyone to leave the house and we stood outside. I had contacted the control room and asked for the local vicar to be turned out and meet us at the house.

While we all stood outside, I took out my truncheon and rapped on the wall of the house with a distinct pattern of knocks. The banging stopped for a moment and started again repeating exactly my pattern of knocks. I did this again with a different pattern and the same thing happened before the persistent and frenzied banging started again.

When the vicar arrived, I explained what was happening although he could hear the noise from outside himself. He asked that the constable and I go with him into the bedroom and pray. My colleague was a Catholic and I had noticed that he had crossed himself more than once during our time at the house. Once inside the bedroom, the vicar called upon the spirit to leave and he prayed. The banging became louder and louder but the vicar calmly continued praying until the noise subsided into silence.

The little girl went back to bed and after a short time her mother called to her and asked her to come downstairs. This time there was no banging and it seemed that the spirit had left. Back at the police station, I recorded what had happened in the occurrence book, commenting that I would expect the Superintendent to think it was all in my imagination. Sure enough, when I arrived for duty the following night the Superintendent was waiting for me to see if I was all right.

Like me, the constable I attended with, never discussed this incident again.

Kingstanding, Birmingham

In the early 1990s I was posted to a panda covering the Kingstanding area to the north of Birmingham. The name is medieval and derives from its later use as a 'standing' which is a grassy mound situated on the Kingstanding Road. This was a place where the king could wait to have deer driven past so that he could hunt with a fair chance of success. Locally, most people think the name comes from the English Civil War, when King Charles I is said to have addressed his troops from the mound. This may have occurred but the name of the mound certainly pre-dates this event. Whatever the origins of the name, it is a mainly residential area consisting of extensive housing estates, which were built from 1928 onwards. From a policing perspective it is a busy area with plenty of work to do.

In the early hours of the morning, a call came through reporting that a woman was being attacked in a house in Streatham Grove. The call had been made from the next-door neighbours who reported that they could hear the assault taking place. I arrived at the location and everything seemed to be quiet. There were no lights on or any noise coming from the house where the incident was believed to be.

I went to the callers address and spoke to the two women who lived there. They explained to me that they had heard shouting and banging coming from the house next door. The house was a semi-detached house and there was a very elderly lady who lived alone. They were clearly very concerned about what they had heard as they were certain that the sound was that of a violent incident

I went next door and hammered on the door. Everything was quiet and there was no sign of a forced entry. Eventually, the door was answered by an old lady who had I had clearly woken up. She seemed bemused to see a police officer standing at her door and I told her the reason why I was there. I explained that her neighbours were very concerned about what they had heard and called the police.

The lady was clearly safe and well and had not been attacked. I asked if she had left the television or radio on before she had gone to bed, she assured me that she had not. Very calmly, the lady explained she had been having some problems with malevolent spirits and that a priest was going to come round and exorcise the house in the next few days.

I wished her a goodnight and went round to explain to the callers about what the lady told me. They were obviously shocked about the reason given for all the commotion. Probably not the best piece of reassurance policing I have undertaken, but at least I had told them the truth.

I could not get away from the house quickly enough.

Keele Services, Staffordshire

Sometime around 1990 I was working as a divisional controller in Staffordshire Police. In those days, any calls that were made from motorway service stations were diverted to us as any crime matters that took place there, requiring a degree of local investigation, were not things that traffic officers enjoyed doing very much. Any calls about incidents on the carriageway would go to our HQ and would be assigned to motorway/traffic resources.

One horrible rainy night, when I was grateful to be working indoors, I took a call from a male motorist who was calling from Keele Services. It was in the early hours of the morning and the man was very distressed, bordering on being hysterical.

I managed to calm him down enough to record the incident he was trying to report. The man told me that he had picked up a motorcyclist, standing in the pouring rain, on a motorway slip road. He described him as being dressed in all black clothing and he had been standing next to an old Norton motorcycle holding a petrol can. The motorcyclist sat alongside him in the front seat and he agreed to give him a lift to the next service station for some petrol. As he pulled off the motorway, he turned to speak to the man who had vanished. The car had not stopped at any point and was still travelling when the man disappeared. Totally beside himself, the man called the police. I despatched two officers who went to the services and spoke to the man, who repeated the same story to them. There were no concerns about the caller and it seemed that he was a genuine, decent bloke. All the officers could do was calm him down as best they could but they were as baffled as me about what was being reported.

The log was closed with 'nothing calling for police action' but it certainly sent shivers up my spine. I am aware of similar stories where other officers have been sent to a male hitchhiking in old motorcycle gear, including goggles, but have found no trace of the man. It is certainly a call that I will never forget.

St Mary and St Margaret's Church, Castle Bromwich

On Halloween night in 1986, I was a young constable posted to plain clothes duty with another officer. We were tasked with the job of paying close attention to St Mary and St Margaret's Church in Castle Bromwich. This is about five miles from Birmingham city centre. The current church was rebuilt around 1726. Unusually, the old church was not demolished and the current church has been built around the old timber framed building creating a 'church within a church.'

There had been some information passed to the police that someone was going to break into the church and sacrifice an animal on the altar. During the previous night, the church had been broken into although nothing had been stolen. In view of this, the intelligence was being taken very seriously. There was nothing subtle about the job that we had been told to do, we were just dropped off and expected to tuck ourselves away in the vicinity of the church. We were both young in service and just had to get on with it.

The church is situated in a dead end and has a small graveyard alongside it, separated by a narrow road and there is only one way in and out. At that time it was popular with courting couples and we had to move few on while we were there. We did not want to be spoilsports but if there was going to be a satanic ritual take place; we wanted to catch the offenders and cars parked up in the vicinity might have put them off.

We waited around in the cold and damp, when not long after midnight, we saw two dark figures in the graveyard. I could not make out whether they were male or female but one of them was discernibly taller than the other. We watched them for a few moments, waiting to see if they would start making their way towards the church building but they just disappeared.

My colleague and I made our way over to the graveyard and in a few moments we established that there was nobody else in there. If you stand in the graveyard by the parapet wall, you can see the Castle Hill on the other side of the Chelmsley Wood Collector Road (A452). It is known locally as Pimple Hill because of its small size. When the road network was developed, there was a lot of archaeological work on the site and it is believed that in Norman times there was a